Splish, Splash, and Blue

by Christianne C. Jones   illustrated by Todd Ouren

Special thanks to our advisers for their expertise:

Linda Frichtel, Design Adjunct Faculty
Minneapolis College of Art & Design

Susan Kesselring, M.A., Literacy Educator
Rosemount–Apple Valley–Eagan (Minnesota) School District

PICTURE WINDOW BOOKS
Minneapolis, Minnesota

Editor: Jill Kalz
Designer: Amy Muehlenhardt
Page Production: Brandie Shoemaker
Art Director: Nathan Gassman
The illustrations in this book were created digitally.

Picture Window Books
5115 Excelsior Boulevard
Suite 232
Minneapolis, MN 55416
877-845-8392
www.picturewindowbooks.com

Printed in the United States of America.

Library of Congress Cataloging-in-Publication Data
Jones, Christianne C.
Splish, splash, and blue / by Christianne C. Jones ;
illustrated by Todd Ouren.
p. cm. — (Know your colors)
Includes bibliographical references and index.
ISBN-13: 978-1-4048-3106-3 (library binding)
ISBN-10: 1-4048-3106-1 (library binding)
ISBN-13: 978-1-4048-3489-7 (paperback)
ISBN-10: 1-4048-3489-3 (paperback)
1. Blue—Juvenile literature. 2. Colors—Juvenile literature.
3. Toy and movable books—Specimens. I. Ouren, Todd, ill.
II. Title.
QC495.5.J66 2007
535.6—dc22   2006027240

The world is filled with COLORS.

BLUE

PURPLE

GREEN

RED

YELLOW

ORANGE

Colors are either primary or secondary. Red, yellow, and blue are primary colors. These are the colors that can't be made by mixing two other colors together. Orange, purple, and green are secondary colors. Secondary colors are made by mixing together two primary colors.

Primary colors   Secondary colors

 =

Blue + Red   Purple

 =

Blue + Yellow   Green

 =

Yellow + Red   Orange

Black and white are neutral colors. They are used to make other colors lighter or darker.

Keep your eyes open for colorful fun!

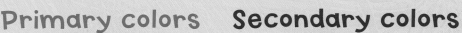

The color **BLUE** can splish, splash, and spray.

4

A water park is cool on a hot summer day.

The clear **BLUE** sky makes everybody grin.

A helpful **BLUE** bottle protects the skin.

9

BLUE plastic buckets are filled to the top.

10

A twisting **BLUE** slide zigzags and drops.

13

A thin **BLUE** mat zooms down the slide.

14